WHSmith

Quick Revision

KS1: Age 5–6

Spelling

Louis Fidge

First published 2007
exclusively for WHSmith by
Hodder Education, an Hachette UK Company, 338 Euston Road,
London NW1 3BH

Impression number 10 9 8 7 6 5 4 3 2
Year 2010 2009

A CIP record for this book is available from the British Library.

Cover illustration: Sally Newton Illustrations

Typeset by Fakenham Photosetting Limited, Fakenham, Norfolk

ISBN 978 0 340 94904 7

Printed and bound in the UK by Hobbs the Printers.

For parents

Quick Revision: Spelling

- Spelling is a key feature of the National Curriculum and the National Literacy Framework.
- Children need to be able to spell in order to read and write fluently and confidently.
- Good spelling is essential in all areas of the curriculum.
- Learning to spell requires constant practice and reinforcement.
- This series of 'teach and test' books will help build your child's confidence and ability in spelling.

Features of the books

- Each unit:
  - has a clear spelling focus
  - introduces ten words which contain the same spelling focus
  - has a range of activities which help your child to learn to spell the words
  - finishes with a spelling test, using the ten Test words.
- Answers to the activities may be found on pages 24–27.
- A record sheet is provided on page 3 on which your child can keep a record of all test scores.

How to do the units

- Do one spelling unit and test each week.
- Agree on a set time with your child, and keep it the same each week if possible.
- Ensure your child can read the Test words at the top of the page and knows their meanings.
- Encourage your child to do the activities to help learn the words.
- On completion of the activities, get your child to do the unit test.

How to do the spelling tests

- Turn to pages 28–32 and find the appropriate answer sheet to complete.
- Ask your child to look back at the Test words in the unit and study these again for a short while.
- Then either:
  - copy out the words and read them slowly to your child (or get another adult or child to read them)

  or:
  - ask your child to write the words from memory (without copying them!)
- When the spelling test has been completed, ask your child to mark it by referring back to the Test words and checking their spellings.
- Colour in the score out of ten.
- After each test, ask your child to fill in the results on the record sheet on page 3.

Spelling test record sheet

Score

10																				
9																				
8																				
7																				
6																				
5																				
4																				
3																				
2																				
1																				
	1	2	3	4	5	6	7	8	9	10	11	12	13	14	15	16	17	18	19	20

Test

Unit 1: Initial letter sounds

Test words

bus	cat	dig	fog	get
hen	jam	lid	top	mug

1. Read the ten Test words.
   Listen to the sound of the letter at the beginning of each word.

2. Write the word that begins with:

   a) d*ig* **b)** g___ **c)** b___ **d)** t___ **e)** c___

   f) f___ **g)** m___ **h)** l___ **i)** j___ **j)** h___

3. Choose the correct letter to begin each word.

a) b g *bus*	**b)** d c ___at	**c)** d m ___ig
d) k f ___og	**e)** r g ___et	**f)** h j ___en
g) j n ___am	**h)** p l ___id	**i)** t r ___op
j) w n ___ug		

4. Now do **Spelling Test 1** on page 28.

Unit 2: Final letter sounds

Test words

peg	beg	map	cap	sit
hit	fox	box	run	fun

1. Read the ten Test words.
   Listen to the sound of the letter at the end of each word.

2. Write the two words that end with:

   a) t ________ ________ **b)** x ________ ________

   c) g ________ ________ **d)** n ________ ________

   e) p ________ ________

3. Choose the correct letter to end each word.

a) b g peg	**b)** g f be__	**c)** p j ma__
d) s p ca__	**e)** t z si__	**f)** h t hi__
g) f x fo__	**h)** x k bo__	**i)** n d ru__
j) n m fu__		

4. Now do **Spelling Test 2** on page 28.

Unit 3: CVC* words with medial **a**

Test words

f_a_t	r__t	d__d	s__d	r__g
b__g	m__n	v__n	t__p	l__p

*Note: CVC = consonant/vowel/consonant

1. Write the missing **a** in each word in the box above. Read the ten Test words you make.

2. Write the word that rhymes with:

   a) rat ____________ **b)** sad ____________

   c) bag ____________ **d)** van ____________

   e) tap ____________

3. Write the word that begins with:

   a) s ____________ **b)** v ____________ **c)** t ____________

   d) l ____________ **e)** f ____________ **f)** d ____________

   g) b ____________ **h)** m ____________

4. Write the two words that begin with r ________ ________

5. Now do **Spelling Test 3** on page 28.

Unit 4: CVC words with medial **e**

Test words

r__d	b__d	h__n	m__n	t__n
g__t	w__t	v__t	y__t	m__t

1. Write the missing **e** in each word in the box above. Read the ten Test words you make.

2. Write the words that end with:

   a) ed ______ ______

   b) en ______ ______ ______

   c) et ______ ______ ______ ______ ______

3. Write the word that begins with:

   a) h ______ **b)** t ______ **c)** r ______ **d)** w ______

   e) v ______ **f)** y ______ **g)** g ______ **h)** b ______

4. Write the words that begin with m ______ ______

5. Underline the Test words in these sentences:

   a) The ten men had a hen. **b)** I have a red bed.

   c) You get wet in the rain. **d)** Have you met the vet yet?

6. Now do **Spelling Test 4** on page 28.

Unit 5: CVC words with medial **i**

Test words

w__n	p__n	h__d	l__d	w__g
b__g	z__p	l__p	f__x	m__x

1. Write the missing **i** in each word in the box above. Read the ten Test words you make.

2. Write the words that end with:

ig	in	ip	ix	id

3. Write the word that begins with:

a) b ________ **b)** f ___________ **c)** h ___________

d) m ________ **e)** p ___________ **f)** z ___________

4. Write the words that begin with:

a) l ___________ ______________

b) w ___________ ______________

5. Now do **Spelling Test 5** on page 29.

Unit 6: CVC words with medial **o**

Test words

j__b	r__b	f__g	l__g	h__p
m__p	c__t	h__t	b__x	f__x

1 Write the missing **o** in each word in the box above. Read the ten Test words you make.

2 Change some letters. Read the new words you make.

a) Change the **j** in **j**ob to **r** *rob*

b) Change the **f** in **f**og to **l** ______

c) Change the **h** in **h**op to **m** ______

d) Change the **c** in **c**ot to **h** ______

e) Change the **b** in **b**ox to **f** ______

f) Change the **r** in **r**ob to **j** ______

g) Change the **l** in **l**og to **f** ______

h) Change the **m** in **m**op to **h** ______

i) Change the **h** in **h**ot to **c** ______

j) Change the **f** in **f**ox to **b** ______

3 Now do **Spelling Test 6** on page 29.

Unit 7: CVC words with medial **u**

Test words

c__b	t__b	j__g	m__g	h__m
m__m	f__n	s__n	h__t	n__t

1. Write the missing **u** in each word in the box above. Read the ten Test words you make.

2. Write the word that rhymes with:
   a) nut ________ **b)** mug ________
   c) tub ________ **d)** sun ________
   e) hum ________

3. Write the word that begins with:
   a) j ________ **b)** n ________ **c)** c ________
   d) f ________ **e)** s ________ **f)** t ________

4. Write the words that begin with:
   a) m ________ ________ **b)** h ________ ________

5. Underline the Test words in these sentences.
   a) It's fun in the sun. **b)** I ate a nut in the hut.
   c) I like to hum with my mum.
   d) The cub fell into the tub.
   e) I poured some milk from the jug into my mug.

6. Now do **Spelling Test 7** on page 29.

Unit 8: ch

Test words

___at	___ip	___op	___in	___ick
ri___	mun___	lun___	pun___	bun___

1. Write the missing **ch** in each word in the box above. Read the ten Test words you make.

2. Fill in the chart.

words beginning with **ch**	words ending with **ch**

3. Choose the correct word to complete each sentence.
   a) You eat a ________ (chat, chip).
   b) You ________ (chop, chin) wood with an axe.
   c) If you are ________ (chick, rich) you have a lot of money.
   d) I ate some pizza for my ________ (lunch, munch).
   e) I gave my mum a ________ (punch, bunch) of flowers.

4. Now do **Spelling Test 8** on page 29.

Unit 9: sh

Test words

___ip	___op	___ut	___ell	___ed
ru___	hu___	fi___	wi___	di___

1. Write the missing **sh** in each word in the box above. Read the ten Test words you make.

2. Fill in the chart.

words beginning with **sh**	words ending with **sh**

3. Choose the correct word to complete each sentence.
   a) A ________ (ship, shop) sails on the sea.
   b) A snail has a ________ (shut, shell).
   c) There is a ________ (shed, rush) in the garden.
   d) I ate some ________ (hush, fish) for my lunch.
   e) I ________ (wish, dish) I was rich!

4. Now do **Spelling Test 9** on page 30.

Unit 10: th

Test words

___ick	___in	___ink	___ud	___ree
wi___	pa___	ba___	mo___	clo___

1. Write the missing **th** in each word in the box above. Read the ten Test words you make.

2. Fill in the chart.

words beginning with **th**	words ending with **th**

3. Choose the correct word to complete each sentence.

a) The bread was very ________ (thin, think).

b) I ate ________ (thick, three) sweets.

c) I went to play ________ (thud, with) my friend.

d) I had a ________ (bath, path) and went to bed.

e) A _______ (moth, cloth) is like a butterfly.

4. Now do **Spelling Test 10** on page 30.

Unit 11: -ll

Test words

ba__	se__	hi__	do__	ye__
tro__	fu__	wa__	pu__	mi__

1. Write the missing **ll** at the end of each word in the box above. Read the ten Test words you make.

2. Write the word that rhymes with:
   a) wall ________ **b)** yell ________
   c) mill ________ **d)** doll ________
   e) full ________

3. Write the word that begins with:
   a) b _____ **b)** d _____ **c)** f _____ **d)** h _____
   e) m _____ **f)** p _____ **g)** s _____ **h)** t _____
   i) w _____ **j)** y _____

4. Choose the correct word for each sentence.
   a) You catch a ________ (ball, wall).
   b) You ________ (sell, yell) loudly.
   c) A ________ (hill, mill) is steep.
   d) A ________ (doll, troll) is ugly.
   e) The glass is ________ (full, pull).

5. Now do **Spelling Test 11** on page 30.

Unit 12: -ck

Test words

ba___	pe___	ki___	ro___	sa___
li___	clo___	du___	ne___	tru___

1. Write the missing **ck** at the end of each word in the box above. Read the ten Test words you make.

2. Write the word that rhymes with:
   a) sack ________ **b)** neck ________
   c) lick ________ **d)** truck ________
   e) rock ________

3. Write the word that begins with:
   a) b _____ **b)** c _____ **c)** d _____ **d)** k _____
   e) l _____ **f)** n _____ **g)** p _____ **h)** r _____
   i) s _____ **j)** t _____

4. Choose the correct word for each sentence.
   a) You ________ (lick, kick) a ball.
   b) A _______ (rock, clock) has hands.
   c) A bird can ________ (neck, peck).
   d) A _______ (duck, truck) can quack.
   e) You put things in a _______ (back, sack).

5. Now do **Spelling Test 12** on page 30.

Unit 13: -ng

Test words

ba___	sa___	ki___	sti___	ri___
wi___	lo___	so___	hu___	lu___

1. Write the missing **ng** at the end of each word in the box above.
   Read the ten Test words you make.

2. Fill in the chart.

ang words	**ing** words	**ong** words	**ung** words

3. Underline the **ng** words in the sentences.
   a) The king sang a long song.
   b) The door shut with a loud bang.
   c) A bird has a wing and a bee can sting.
   d) I hung my picture on the wall.
   e) You can ring a bell.
   f) A lung helps you to breathe.

4. Now do **Spelling Test 13** on page 31.

Unit 14: ea

Test words

s___	t___	___t	___ch	s___t
m___l	b___k	cl___n	r___d	b___ch

1. Write the missing **ea** in each word in the box above. Read the ten Test words you make.

2. Fill in the chart with words which:

begin with **ea**	end with **ea**	have **ea** in the middle

3. Choose the correct word for each sentence.

   a) You swim in the ________ (sea, tea).

   b) If you are hungry you ________ (eat, each).

   c) You sit on a ________ (seat, meal).

   d) A bird has a ________ (beak, clean).

   e) You ________ (beach, read) a book.

4. Now do **Spelling Test 14** on page 31.

Unit 15: ee

Test words

b___	s___	tr___	thr___	n___d
w___k	f___t	sl___p	p___l	gr___n

1. Write the missing **ee** in each word in the box above. Read the ten Test words you make.

2. Fill in the chart with words which:

end with **ee**	have **ee** in the middle

3. Which words:

a) have three letters? ________ ________

b) have four letters? ________ ________ ________

________ ________

c) have five letters? ________ ________ ________

4. Now do **Spelling Test 15** on page 31.

Unit 16: **ay**

Test words

d___	m___	l___	s___	w___
cl___	pl___	tr___	st___	spr___

1. Write the missing **ay** at the end of each word in the box above. Read the ten Test words you make.

2. Change some letters. Read the new words you make.

   a) Change the **d** in **d**ay to **m** *may*

   b) Change the **m** in **m**ay to **l** ________

   c) Change the **l** in **l**ay to **s** ________

   d) Change the **s** in **s**ay to **w** ________

   e) Change the **w** in **w**ay to **cl** ________

   f) Change the **cl** in **cl**ay to **pl** ________

   g) Change the **pl** in **pl**ay to **tr** ________

   h) Change the **tr** in **tr**ay to **st** ________

   i) Change the **st** in **st**ay to **spr** ________

   j) Change the **spr** in **spr**ay to **d** ________

3. Now do **Spelling Test 16** on page 31.

Unit 17: **ai**

Test words

r____n	p____l	j____l	tr____n	dr____n
s____l	br____n	ch____n	n____l	t____l

1. Write the missing **ai** in each word in the box above. Read the ten Test words you make.

2. Fill in the chart.

ain words	**ail** words

3. Choose the correct word for each sentence.
   a) You get wet in the __________ (rain, train).
   b) You hit a _________ (jail, nail) with a hammer.
   c) You _________ (pail, sail) on a boat.
   d) You think with your __________ (brain, drain).
   e) A rat has a __________ (chain, tail).

4. Now do **Spelling Test 17** on page 32.

Unit 18: **a–e** (magic **e**)

Test words

mad__	cak__	nam__	lat__	cav__
wav__	hat__	spad__	gam__	rak__

1. Write the magic **e** at the end of each word in the box above. Read the ten Test words you make.

2. Write the word that rhymes with:

   a) made ____________ **b)** cake ____________

   c) name ____________ **d)** late ____________

   e) cave ____________

3. Underline the Test words in the sentences.

   a) I made a cake.

   b) I hate to be late.

   c) In the shed there was a spade and a rake.

   d) A bear lived in the dark cave.

   e) I always wave to my friend when I see her.

   f) My friend's name is Mia.

   g) I played a game with my friend.

4. Now do **Spelling Test 18** on page 32.

Unit 19: Key words (1)

Test words

Monday Tuesday Wednesday Thursday Friday
Saturday Sunday today yesterday holiday

1. Read the ten Test words.

2. Write the day that comes after:

   a) Wednesday ____________

   b) Friday ____________

   c) Sunday ____________

   d) Thursday ____________

   e) Monday ____________

   f) Saturday ____________

   g) Tuesday ____________

3. Write the word that means:

   a) the day before today ____________

   b) the day before tomorrow ____________

   c) a long break from school ____________

4. Now do **Spelling Test 19** on page 32.

Unit 20: Key words (2)

Test words

red	green	blue	black	brown
pink	orange	white	yellow	purple

1. Read the ten Test words.

2. Write the words that contain:

   a) three letters: ________

   b) four letters: ________ ________

   c) five letters: ________ ________ ________ ________

   d) six letters: ________ ________ ________

3. Write the words that begin with:

   a) y ________ **b)** w ________ **c)** r ________

   d) g ________ **e)** o ________

   f) p ________ ________

   g) b ________ ________ ________

4. Now do **Spelling Test 20** on page 32.

Answers

Unit 1

2 a dig b get c bus
d top e cat f fog
g mug h lid i jam
j hen

3 a bus b cat c dig
d fog e get f hen
g jam h lid i top
j mug

Unit 2

2 a sit hit b fox box
c peg beg d run fun
e map cap

3 a peg b beg c map
d cap e sit f hit
g fox h box i run
j fun

Unit 3

1 fat rat dad sad rag
bag man van tap lap

2 a fat b dad c rag
d man e lap

3 a sad b van c tap
d lap e fat f dad
g bag h man

4 rat rag

Unit 4

1 red bed hen men ten
get wet vet yet met

2 a red bed
b hen men ten
c get wet vet yet met

3 a hen b ten c red
d wet e vet f yet
g get h bed

4 men met

5 a The <u>ten</u> <u>men</u> had a <u>hen</u>.
b I have a <u>red</u> <u>bed</u>.
c You <u>get</u> <u>wet</u> in the rain.
d Have you <u>met</u> the <u>vet</u> <u>yet</u>?

Unit 5

1 win pin hid lid wig
big zip lip fix mix

2 **ig** **in** **ip** **ix** **id**
wig win zip fix hid
big pin lip mix lid

3 a big b fix c hid
d mix e pin f zip

4 a lid lip b wig win

Unit 6

1 job rob fog log hop
mop cot hot box fox

2 a rob b log c mop
d hot e fox f job
g fog h hop i cot
j box

Unit 7

1 cub tub jug mug hum
mum fun sun hut nut

2 a hut b jug c cub
d fun e mum

3 a jug b nut c cub
d fun e sun f tub

4 a mum mug b hum hut

5 a It's <u>fun</u> in the <u>sun</u>.
b I ate a <u>nut</u> in the <u>hut</u>.
c I like to <u>hum</u> with my <u>mum</u>.
d The <u>cub</u> fell into the <u>tub</u>.
e I poured some milk from the <u>jug</u> into my <u>mug</u>.

Unit 8

1 chat chip chop chin
chick rich munch lunch
punch bunch

2 words beginning with **ch**:
chat chip chop chin chick
words ending with **ch**:
rich munch lunch punch bunch

3 a chip b chop c rich
d lunch e bunch

Unit 9

1 ship shop shut shell
shed rush hush fish
wish dish

2 words beginning with **sh**:
ship shop shut shell shed
words ending with **sh**:
rush hush fish wish dish

3 a ship b shell c shed
d fish e wish

Unit 10

1 thick thin think thud
three with path bath
moth cloth

2 words beginning with **th**:
thick thin think thud three
words ending with **th**:
with path bath moth cloth

3 a thin b three c with
d bath e moth

Unit 11

1 ball sell hill doll yell
troll full wall pull mill

2 a ball b sell c hill
d troll e pull

3 a ball b doll c full
d hill e mill f pull
g sell h troll i wall
j yell

4 a ball b yell c hill
d troll e full

Unit 12

1 back peck kick rock
sack lick clock duck
neck truck

2 a back b peck c kick
d duck e clock

3 a back b clock c duck
d kick e lick f neck
g peck h rock i sack
j truck

4 a kick b clock c peck
d duck e sack

Unit 13

1 bang sang king sting
ring wing long song
hung lung

2 **ang** words: bang sang
ing words: king sting ring wing
ong words: long song
ung words: hung, lung

3 a The king sang a long song.
b The door shut with a loud bang.
c A bird has a wing and a bee can sting.
d I hung my picture on the wall.
e You can ring a bell.
f A lung helps you to breathe.

Unit 14

1 sea tea eat each seat
meal beak clean read
beach

2 begin with **ea**: eat each
end with **ea**: sea tea
have **ea** in the middle:
seat meal beak clean read beach

3 a sea b eat c seat
d beak e read

Unit 15

1 bee see tree three
need week feet sleep
peel green

2 end with **ee**: bee see tree three
have **ee** in the middle: need week feet sleep peel green

3 a bee see
b tree need week feet peel
c three sleep green

Unit 16

1 day may lay say way clay play tray stay spray

2 a may b lay c say
d way e clay f play
g tray h stay i spray
j day

Unit 17

1 rain pail jail train drain sail brain chain nail tail

2 **ain** words: rain train drain brain chain
ail words: pail jail sail nail tail

3 a rain b nail c sail
d brain e tail

Unit 18

1 made cake name late cave wave hate spade game rake

2 a spade b rake c game
d hate e wave

3 a I made a cake.
b I hate to be late.
c In the shed there was a spade and a rake.
d A bear lived in the dark cave.
e I always wave to my friend when I see her.
f My friend's name is Mia.
g I played a game with my friend.

Unit 19

2 a Thursday b Saturday
c Monday d Friday
e Tuesday f Sunday
g Wednesday

3 a yesterday b today
c holiday

Unit 20

2 a red b blue pink
c green black brown white
d orange yellow purple

3 a yellow b white c red
d green e orange f pink purple g blue black brown

Spelling test answers

Test 1

1 ____________________
2 ____________________
3 ____________________
4 ____________________
5 ____________________
6 ____________________
7 ____________________
8 ____________________
9 ____________________
10 ____________________

Score ____

Test 2

1 ____________________
2 ____________________
3 ____________________
4 ____________________
5 ____________________
6 ____________________
7 ____________________
8 ____________________
9 ____________________
10 ____________________

Score ____

Test 3

1 ____________________
2 ____________________
3 ____________________
4 ____________________
5 ____________________
6 ____________________
7 ____________________
8 ____________________
9 ____________________
10 ____________________

Score ____

Test 4

1 ____________________
2 ____________________
3 ____________________
4 ____________________
5 ____________________
6 ____________________
7 ____________________
8 ____________________
9 ____________________
10 ____________________

Score ____

Test 5

1 ____________________
2 ____________________
3 ____________________
4 ____________________
5 ____________________
6 ____________________
7 ____________________
8 ____________________
9 ____________________
10 ____________________

Score ____

Test 6

1 ____________________
2 ____________________
3 ____________________
4 ____________________
5 ____________________
6 ____________________
7 ____________________
8 ____________________
9 ____________________
10 ____________________

Score ____

Test 7

1 ____________________
2 ____________________
3 ____________________
4 ____________________
5 ____________________
6 ____________________
7 ____________________
8 ____________________
9 ____________________
10 ____________________

Score ____

Test 8

1 ____________________
2 ____________________
3 ____________________
4 ____________________
5 ____________________
6 ____________________
7 ____________________
8 ____________________
9 ____________________
10 ____________________

Score ____

Test 9

1 ____________________
2 ____________________
3 ____________________
4 ____________________
5 ____________________
6 ____________________
7 ____________________
8 ____________________
9 ____________________
10 ____________________

Score ____

Test 10

1 ____________________
2 ____________________
3 ____________________
4 ____________________
5 ____________________
6 ____________________
7 ____________________
8 ____________________
9 ____________________
10 ____________________

Score ____

Test 11

1 ____________________
2 ____________________
3 ____________________
4 ____________________
5 ____________________
6 ____________________
7 ____________________
8 ____________________
9 ____________________
10 ____________________

Score ____

Test 12

1 ____________________
2 ____________________
3 ____________________
4 ____________________
5 ____________________
6 ____________________
7 ____________________
8 ____________________
9 ____________________
10 ____________________

Score ____

Test 13

1 ______
2 ______
3 ______
4 ______
5 ______
6 ______
7 ______
8 ______
9 ______
10 ______

Score ____

Test 14

1 ______
2 ______
3 ______
4 ______
5 ______
6 ______
7 ______
8 ______
9 ______
10 ______

Score ____

Test 15

1 ______
2 ______
3 ______
4 ______
5 ______
6 ______
7 ______
8 ______
9 ______
10 ______

Score ____

Test 16

1 ______
2 ______
3 ______
4 ______
5 ______
6 ______
7 ______
8 ______
9 ______
10 ______

Score ____

Test 17

1 ______________________________
2 ______________________________
3 ______________________________
4 ______________________________
5 ______________________________
6 ______________________________
7 ______________________________
8 ______________________________
9 ______________________________
10 ______________________________

Score ____

Test 18

1 ______________________________
2 ______________________________
3 ______________________________
4 ______________________________
5 ______________________________
6 ______________________________
7 ______________________________
8 ______________________________
9 ______________________________
10 ______________________________

Score ____

Test 19

1 ______________________________
2 ______________________________
3 ______________________________
4 ______________________________
5 ______________________________
6 ______________________________
7 ______________________________
8 ______________________________
9 ______________________________
10 ______________________________

Score ____

Test 20

1 ______________________________
2 ______________________________
3 ______________________________
4 ______________________________
5 ______________________________
6 ______________________________
7 ______________________________
8 ______________________________
9 ______________________________
10 ______________________________

Score ____